EMMANUEL JOSEPH

The Infinite Portfolio, Innovation, Leadership, and the Billionaire's Playbook for Change

Copyright © 2025 by Emmanuel Joseph

All rights reserved. No part of this publication may be reproduced, stored or transmitted in any form or by any means, electronic, mechanical, photocopying, recording, scanning, or otherwise without written permission from the publisher. It is illegal to copy this book, post it to a website, or distribute it by any other means without permission.

First edition

This book was professionally typeset on Reedsy.
Find out more at reedsy.com

Contents

1	Chapter 1: Unveiling the Vision	1
2	Chapter 2: Embracing Disruption	3
3	Chapter 3: The Power of Collaboration	5
4	Chapter 4: Navigating the Unknown	7
5	Chapter 5: Cultivating Creativity	9
6	Chapter 6: The Role of Technology	11
7	Chapter 7: Building Resilient Organizations	13
8	Chapter 8: The Art of Strategic Thinking	15
9	Chapter 9: Leading with Purpose	17
10	Chapter 10: Empowering Teams	19
11	Chapter 11: The Importance of Ethical Leadership	21
12	Chapter 12: Leading Through Crisis	23
13	Chapter 13: Fostering Innovation Ecosystems	25
14	Chapter 14: The Future of Leadership	27
15	Chapter 15: Leveraging Diversity and Inclusion	29
16	Chapter 16: Sustainability and Environmental Responsibility	31
17	Chapter 17: Legacy and Impact	33

1

Chapter 1: Unveiling the Vision

In the dawn of the 21st century, the world witnessed an unprecedented surge in technological advancements, reshaping industries and economies globally. Within this dynamic landscape emerged a cohort of visionaries who harnessed innovation to not only build empires but to redefine the paradigms of success. This chapter delves into the inception of such transformative visions, dissecting the pivotal moments that sparked revolutionary ideas. The journey begins with a glimpse into the minds of those who dared to dream beyond conventional boundaries, setting the stage for a narrative that weaves ambition with audacity.

The crux of innovation lies in the ability to perceive possibilities where others see obstacles. It is this inherent capability that propelled certain individuals to the forefront of their industries. From the early inklings of groundbreaking concepts to the painstaking process of bringing these ideas to fruition, the path of an innovator is fraught with challenges and triumphs alike. Here, we explore the stories of early pioneers who laid the groundwork for a new era of leadership, highlighting their relentless pursuit of excellence.

As the seeds of innovation took root, a new breed of leaders emerged—ones who not only embraced change but actively sought it. Their leadership styles were characterized by a unique blend of creativity, resilience, and an unwavering commitment to their vision. This chapter examines the traits that set these leaders apart, offering insights into the qualities that fostered their meteoric rise. By dissecting their approaches to problem-solving and decision-making, we gain a deeper understanding of the essence of effective leadership in a rapidly evolving world.

At the heart of this narrative lies the concept of the infinite portfolio—a testament to the boundless potential of innovation and leadership. This portfolio is not confined to financial assets alone; it encompasses a wealth of ideas, strategies, and solutions that drive progress. Through the lens of visionary leaders, we explore the multidimensional aspects of this portfolio, unraveling the intricate interplay between innovation and leadership. As we embark on this journey, we are reminded that the true measure of success lies not in the accumulation of wealth, but in the legacy of transformative change.

2

Chapter 2: Embracing Disruption

In a world where change is the only constant, the ability to embrace disruption becomes a hallmark of true leadership. This chapter delves into the phenomenon of disruption, exploring its impact on industries and the strategies employed by visionary leaders to navigate its complexities. By examining real-world examples, we uncover the mindset required to turn disruption into an opportunity for growth and innovation.

Disruption often arrives unannounced, challenging established norms and forcing organizations to adapt or perish. It is within this crucible of uncertainty that true leaders emerge, demonstrating a remarkable capacity to pivot and thrive. This chapter delves into the stories of those who successfully navigated disruptive forces, showcasing their ability to remain agile and resilient in the face of adversity. Through their experiences, we glean valuable lessons on the art of embracing change and leveraging it to drive progress.

Central to the ability to embrace disruption is a culture of innovation that permeates every level of an organization. Visionary leaders understand that fostering an environment where creativity and experimentation are encouraged is essential for sustained success. By examining the practices and philosophies of these leaders, we gain insights into the importance of cultivating a culture that not only tolerates but celebrates disruption. This chapter explores the role of organizational culture in driving innovation, highlighting the ways in which it shapes the trajectory of change.

THE INFINITE PORTFOLIO, INNOVATION, LEADERSHIP, AND THE BILLIONAIRE'S PLAYBOOK FOR CHANGE

At the intersection of innovation and disruption lies the concept of the infinite portfolio—a dynamic repository of ideas and strategies that enable leaders to stay ahead of the curve. This portfolio is constantly evolving, reflecting the ever-changing landscape of opportunities and challenges. Through the lens of visionary leaders, we delve into the ways in which they harness the power of disruption to fuel their infinite portfolios, driving their organizations toward continued growth and success.

3

Chapter 3: The Power of Collaboration

In an interconnected world, the power of collaboration emerges as a pivotal force in driving innovation and achieving transformative change. This chapter explores the dynamics of collaboration, examining how visionary leaders leverage partnerships and networks to amplify their impact. Through compelling case studies, we uncover the strategies employed by these leaders to foster collaboration and harness its potential.

Collaboration is more than just a buzzword; it is a fundamental driver of progress in the modern era. Visionary leaders understand that the most significant breakthroughs often result from the convergence of diverse perspectives and expertise. This chapter delves into the stories of those who have mastered the art of collaboration, highlighting their ability to forge alliances and build networks that transcend traditional boundaries. By examining their approaches, we gain insights into the mechanisms that facilitate successful collaboration and the tangible benefits it brings.

At the core of effective collaboration lies the ability to build and nurture relationships based on trust and mutual respect. Visionary leaders recognize that strong relationships are the bedrock of any successful partnership. This chapter explores the importance of relationship-building in the context of collaboration, offering practical insights into the strategies employed by leaders to cultivate and maintain these vital connections. Through their experiences, we learn how to navigate the complexities of collaborative endeavors and unlock their full potential.

The infinite portfolio is enriched through the power of collaboration, as it brings together a diverse array of ideas, perspectives, and resources. Visionary leaders understand that their portfolios are not confined to individual capabilities but are amplified through collective efforts. This chapter delves into the ways in which collaboration enhances the infinite portfolio, driving innovation and enabling leaders to achieve greater impact.

4

Chapter 4: Navigating the Unknown

Innovation often requires venturing into uncharted territories, where uncertainty and risk are inherent. This chapter delves into the mindset and strategies employed by visionary leaders to navigate the unknown, embracing uncertainty as a catalyst for growth. Through captivating narratives, we uncover the experiences of those who have successfully charted new paths and pushed the boundaries of what is possible.

The journey of innovation is rarely linear; it is marked by twists, turns, and unexpected challenges. Visionary leaders understand that navigating the unknown requires a unique blend of courage, resilience, and adaptability. This chapter explores the stories of those who have ventured into uncharted waters, highlighting their ability to remain steadfast in the face of uncertainty. By examining their approaches to risk-taking and decision-making, we gain valuable insights into the art of navigating the unknown.

Central to the ability to navigate the unknown is a willingness to embrace failure as a learning opportunity. Visionary leaders recognize that setbacks and mistakes are an inevitable part of the innovation process. This chapter delves into the importance of cultivating a growth mindset, where failures are viewed as stepping stones to success. Through the experiences of these leaders, we learn how to harness the power of resilience and turn adversity into an opportunity for growth.

The infinite portfolio thrives in the face of uncertainty, as it is continuously shaped by the dynamic forces of innovation and change. Visionary leaders understand that the unknown is not to be feared, but to be embraced as a source of inspiration and growth. This chapter explores the ways in which leaders leverage the unknown to enrich their infinite portfolios, driving their organizations toward new horizons.

5

Chapter 5: Cultivating Creativity

Creativity is the lifeblood of innovation, fueling the development of new ideas and solutions. This chapter delves into the essence of creativity, examining the ways in which visionary leaders foster and harness creative thinking within their organizations. Through engaging stories and practical insights, we uncover the mechanisms that enable leaders to cultivate a culture of creativity.

Creativity thrives in environments where curiosity and experimentation are encouraged. Visionary leaders understand that fostering a culture of creativity requires more than just lip service; it demands a commitment to creating spaces where individuals feel empowered to explore and innovate. This chapter explores the practices and philosophies that underpin such environments, highlighting the importance of nurturing creative potential at every level of an organization.

At the heart of creativity lies the ability to think beyond conventional boundaries and challenge the status quo. Visionary leaders recognize that true innovation often emerges from questioning established norms and embracing unconventional ideas. This chapter delves into the stories of those who have dared to think differently, showcasing their ability to transform radical concepts into tangible outcomes. By examining their approaches, we gain valuable insights into the art of thinking outside the box.

The infinite portfolio is enriched by a continuous influx of creative ideas and solutions. Visionary leaders understand that their portfolios are not static; they are dynamic repositories that evolve with the ever-changing landscape of innovation. This chapter explores the ways in which leaders harness creativity to expand their infinite portfolios, driving their organizations toward new heights.

6

Chapter 6: The Role of Technology

Technology serves as a powerful catalyst for innovation, enabling visionary leaders to push the boundaries of what is possible. This chapter explores the intersection of technology and leadership, examining how cutting-edge advancements have reshaped industries and driven transformative change. Through compelling narratives, we uncover the ways in which leaders leverage technology to build their infinite portfolios.

The rapid pace of technological advancement presents both opportunities and challenges for leaders. Visionary leaders understand that staying ahead of the curve requires a keen understanding of emerging technologies and their potential applications. This chapter delves into the stories of those who have successfully harnessed technology to drive innovation, highlighting their ability to anticipate trends and adapt to new realities. By examining their approaches, we gain valuable insights into the role of technology in shaping the future.

At the core of technological innovation lies the ability to integrate new tools and systems into existing frameworks. Visionary leaders recognize that technology is not an end in itself, but a means to achieve greater impact. This chapter explores the importance of strategic integration, offering practical insights into the ways in which leaders effectively incorporate technology into their organizations. Through their experiences, we learn how to navigate the complexities of technological adoption and maximize its potential.

The infinite portfolio is continually enriched by technological advancements, reflecting the dynamic nature of innovation. Visionary leaders understand that their portfolios must evolve in tandem with technological progress, ensuring that they remain at the forefront of change. This chapter delves into the ways in which leaders leverage technology to expand their infinite portfolios, driving their organizations toward sustained success.

7

Chapter 7: Building Resilient Organizations

Resilience is a crucial attribute for organizations navigating the complexities of a rapidly changing world. This chapter explores the concept of organizational resilience, examining the strategies employed by visionary leaders to build and sustain resilient enterprises. Through engaging narratives, we uncover the mechanisms that enable organizations to thrive in the face of adversity.

Resilient organizations are characterized by their ability to adapt and respond to challenges with agility and strength. Visionary leaders understand that building resilience requires a proactive approach to identifying and mitigating risks. This chapter delves into the stories of those who have successfully navigated crises, showcasing their ability to remain steadfast and resilient. By examining their approaches, we gain valuable insights into the art of building resilient organizations.

At the heart of organizational resilience lies the ability to foster a culture of trust and collaboration. Visionary leaders recognize that strong relationships and a sense of shared purpose are essential for navigating challenges. This chapter explores the importance of cultivating a supportive and collaborative environment, offering practical insights into the strategies employed by leaders to build resilience within their teams. Through their experiences, we learn how to harness the power of collective strength to overcome adversity.

The infinite portfolio is enriched by the resilience of the organizations that embody it, reflecting the dynamic interplay between innovation and stability. Visionary leaders understand that their portfolios must be adaptable and resilient, ensuring that they can withstand the pressures of change. This chapter delves into the ways in which leaders build resilient organizations to sustain their infinite portfolios, driving their enterprises toward continued growth and success.

8

Chapter 8: The Art of Strategic Thinking

Strategic thinking is a cornerstone of effective leadership, enabling visionary leaders to chart a course toward long-term success. This chapter delves into the essence of strategic thinking, examining the ways in which leaders formulate and execute strategies to achieve their goals. Through engaging narratives, we uncover the processes that underpin strategic decision-making and the impact it has on organizational outcomes.

Strategic thinking involves a holistic approach to understanding the complex interplay between various factors that influence success. Visionary leaders recognize the importance of aligning their strategies with their overarching vision, ensuring that every decision contributes to their long-term objectives. This chapter explores the stories of those who have mastered the art of strategic thinking, highlighting their ability to anticipate trends, identify opportunities, and navigate challenges. By examining their approaches, we gain valuable insights into the principles of effective strategy formulation.

At the heart of strategic thinking lies the ability to balance short-term needs with long-term aspirations. Visionary leaders understand that achieving sustainable success requires a careful balance between immediate actions and future goals. This chapter delves into the importance of maintaining a dual focus, offering practical insights into the ways in which leaders strike this balance. Through their experiences, we learn how to craft strategies that are both responsive to current realities and aligned with future aspirations.

The infinite portfolio thrives on strategic thinking, as it provides a framework for navigating the ever-changing landscape of innovation and change. Visionary leaders understand that their portfolios must be guided by a clear and coherent strategy, ensuring that they remain agile and adaptable. This chapter explores the ways in which leaders leverage strategic thinking to expand their infinite portfolios, driving their organizations toward sustained success.

9

Chapter 9: Leading with Purpose

Purpose-driven leadership is a defining characteristic of visionary leaders, guiding their actions and decisions toward meaningful impact. This chapter explores the concept of purpose-driven leadership, examining how leaders align their values and vision with their organizational goals. Through compelling narratives, we uncover the ways in which purpose-driven leaders inspire and motivate their teams to achieve greatness.

Purpose-driven leadership is rooted in a deep sense of mission and commitment to making a positive difference. Visionary leaders understand that true success is not measured solely by financial performance, but by the extent to which they contribute to the greater good. This chapter delves into the stories of those who lead with purpose, highlighting their ability to create a sense of meaning and direction within their organizations. By examining their approaches, we gain valuable insights into the principles of purpose-driven leadership.

At the core of purpose-driven leadership lies the ability to inspire and engage others in the pursuit of a shared vision. Visionary leaders recognize that their success is contingent upon the collective efforts of their teams. This chapter explores the importance of fostering a sense of ownership and alignment among team members, offering practical insights into the strategies employed by leaders to build cohesive and motivated teams. Through their experiences, we learn how to cultivate a culture of purpose that drives organizational success.

The infinite portfolio is enriched by a strong sense of purpose, as it provides a guiding framework for innovation and growth. Visionary leaders understand that their portfolios must be aligned with their values and vision, ensuring that every action contributes to their overarching mission. This chapter delves into the ways in which leaders integrate purpose into their infinite portfolios, driving their organizations toward meaningful impact.

10

Chapter 10: Empowering Teams

Empowering teams is a fundamental aspect of effective leadership, enabling organizations to harness the full potential of their talent. This chapter explores the dynamics of team empowerment, examining how visionary leaders create environments where individuals feel valued, motivated, and empowered to contribute. Through engaging narratives, we uncover the mechanisms that facilitate team empowerment and its impact on organizational success.

Empowering teams involves more than just delegating tasks; it requires creating a culture of trust, collaboration, and mutual respect. Visionary leaders understand that empowering individuals to take ownership of their work fosters a sense of accountability and commitment. This chapter delves into the stories of those who have successfully empowered their teams, highlighting their ability to create environments where innovation and creativity thrive. By examining their approaches, we gain valuable insights into the principles of team empowerment.

At the heart of team empowerment lies the ability to provide the necessary support and resources for individuals to succeed. Visionary leaders recognize that empowering teams requires a commitment to continuous development and growth. This chapter explores the importance of investing in the professional and personal development of team members, offering practical insights into the strategies employed by leaders to nurture talent. Through their experiences, we learn how to create a culture of empowerment that drives organizational success.

The infinite portfolio is enriched by the collective contributions of empowered teams, reflecting the dynamic interplay between individual and organizational growth. Visionary leaders understand that their portfolios are not limited to their own capabilities but are amplified through the talents and efforts of their teams. This chapter delves into the ways in which leaders harness team empowerment to expand their infinite portfolios, driving their organizations toward sustained success.

11

Chapter 11: The Importance of Ethical Leadership

Ethical leadership is a cornerstone of responsible and sustainable success, guiding leaders to act with integrity and accountability. This chapter explores the principles of ethical leadership, examining how visionary leaders navigate complex ethical dilemmas and uphold their values. Through compelling narratives, we uncover the ways in which ethical leadership shapes organizational culture and drives long-term success.

Ethical leadership involves more than just adhering to rules and regulations; it requires a commitment to doing what is right, even in the face of difficult choices. Visionary leaders understand that their actions set the tone for their organizations, influencing the behavior and attitudes of their teams. This chapter delves into the stories of those who exemplify ethical leadership, highlighting their ability to navigate challenging situations with integrity and fairness. By examining their approaches, we gain valuable insights into the principles of ethical decision-making.

At the core of ethical leadership lies the ability to foster a culture of transparency and accountability. Visionary leaders recognize that ethical behavior must be embedded in the fabric of their organizations, shaping the way decisions are made and actions are taken. This chapter explores the importance of creating an environment where ethical considerations are prioritized, offering practical insights into the strategies employed by leaders to build a culture of integrity. Through their experiences, we learn how to navigate ethical challenges and uphold the highest standards of conduct.

The infinite portfolio is enriched by a strong foundation of ethical leadership, ensuring that innovation and growth are pursued responsibly and sustainably. Visionary leaders understand that their portfolios must be built on a foundation of trust and integrity, ensuring that their actions contribute to the greater good. This chapter delves into the ways in which leaders integrate ethical considerations into their infinite portfolios, driving their organizations toward long-term success.

12

Chapter 12: Leading Through Crisis

Crisis situations are inevitable in the world of leadership, and how leaders respond to these challenges can define their legacy. This chapter explores the art of leading through crisis, examining the strategies employed by visionary leaders to navigate turbulent times. Through compelling narratives, we uncover the ways in which leaders demonstrate resilience, decisiveness, and compassion in the face of adversity.

Leading through crisis requires a unique set of skills and attributes. Visionary leaders understand that their actions during a crisis can have a profound impact on their organizations and stakeholders. This chapter delves into the stories of those who have successfully led their teams through challenging situations, highlighting their ability to remain calm, focused, and adaptable. By examining their approaches, we gain valuable insights into the principles of effective crisis leadership.

At the heart of crisis leadership lies the ability to communicate with transparency and empathy. Visionary leaders recognize that clear and compassionate communication is essential for maintaining trust and morale during difficult times. This chapter explores the importance of effective communication in crisis situations, offering practical insights into the strategies employed by leaders to keep their teams informed and motivated. Through their experiences, we learn how to navigate the complexities of crisis communication and build trust in the face of uncertainty.

THE INFINITE PORTFOLIO, INNOVATION, LEADERSHIP, AND THE BILLIONAIRE'S PLAYBOOK FOR CHANGE

The infinite portfolio is fortified by the experiences of leading through crisis, reflecting the lessons learned and the resilience developed. Visionary leaders understand that their portfolios must be adaptable and resilient, capable of withstanding the pressures of crisis situations. This chapter delves into the ways in which leaders leverage their experiences to strengthen their infinite portfolios, driving their organizations toward recovery and growth.

13

Chapter 13: Fostering Innovation Ecosystems

Innovation ecosystems are dynamic environments where ideas, talent, and resources converge to drive progress. This chapter explores the concept of innovation ecosystems, examining how visionary leaders cultivate and nurture these environments to foster innovation. Through engaging narratives, we uncover the strategies employed by leaders to build vibrant ecosystems that support sustainable growth.

Innovation ecosystems thrive on collaboration and the exchange of ideas. Visionary leaders understand that creating a successful ecosystem requires bringing together diverse stakeholders, including entrepreneurs, researchers, investors, and policymakers. This chapter delves into the stories of those who have successfully built and nurtured innovation ecosystems, highlighting their ability to foster collaboration and create synergies. By examining their approaches, we gain valuable insights into the principles of ecosystem development.

At the core of innovation ecosystems lies the ability to create a supportive infrastructure that enables innovation to flourish. Visionary leaders recognize that providing the necessary resources, such as funding, mentorship, and access to networks, is essential for nurturing talent and ideas. This chapter explores the importance of building a robust support system, offering practical insights into the strategies employed by leaders to create conducive environments for innovation. Through their experiences, we learn how to cultivate ecosystems that drive sustainable growth.

The infinite portfolio is enriched by the contributions of innovation ecosystems, reflecting the dynamic interplay between diverse stakeholders and their collective efforts. Visionary leaders understand that their portfolios must be interconnected with broader ecosystems, ensuring that they benefit from the collective intelligence and resources of their networks. This chapter delves into the ways in which leaders leverage innovation ecosystems to expand their infinite portfolios, driving their organizations toward new horizons.

14

Chapter 14: The Future of Leadership

The future of leadership is shaped by the evolving landscape of technology, society, and the global economy. This chapter explores the emerging trends and challenges that will define the future of leadership, examining how visionary leaders prepare for and navigate these changes. Through thought-provoking narratives, we uncover the ways in which leaders anticipate and adapt to the future.

The rapid pace of technological advancement presents both opportunities and challenges for future leaders. Visionary leaders understand that staying ahead of the curve requires a keen understanding of emerging technologies and their potential impact. This chapter delves into the stories of those who are at the forefront of technological innovation, highlighting their ability to anticipate trends and adapt to new realities. By examining their approaches, we gain valuable insights into the future of leadership in a technologically driven world.

At the heart of future leadership lies the ability to navigate the complexities of a globalized and interconnected world. Visionary leaders recognize that the future will be shaped by a diverse array of factors, including geopolitical shifts, environmental challenges, and societal changes. This chapter explores the importance of adopting a holistic and forward-thinking approach, offering practical insights into the strategies employed by leaders to prepare for the future. Through their experiences, we learn how to build resilient and adaptable organizations that can thrive in an ever-changing landscape.

The infinite portfolio is continually evolving, reflecting the dynamic nature of the future. Visionary leaders understand that their portfolios must be adaptable and forward-looking, ensuring that they remain relevant and impactful in the face of change. This chapter delves into the ways in which leaders leverage their vision and foresight to expand their infinite portfolios, driving their organizations toward future success.

15

Chapter 15: Leveraging Diversity and Inclusion

Diversity and inclusion are critical components of a thriving and innovative organization. This chapter explores the importance of leveraging diversity and inclusion, examining how visionary leaders create environments where all individuals feel valued and empowered. Through compelling narratives, we uncover the strategies employed by leaders to build diverse and inclusive organizations.

Diversity brings a wealth of perspectives, experiences, and ideas that drive innovation and creativity. Visionary leaders understand that embracing diversity is essential for achieving sustainable success. This chapter delves into the stories of those who have successfully fostered diversity within their organizations, highlighting their ability to create inclusive cultures where everyone can thrive. By examining their approaches, we gain valuable insights into the principles of diversity and inclusion.

At the core of diversity and inclusion lies the ability to create an environment where all individuals feel a sense of belonging and empowerment. Visionary leaders recognize that building an inclusive culture requires a commitment to equity and respect. This chapter explores the importance of creating a supportive and inclusive environment, offering practical insights into the strategies employed by leaders to foster diversity and inclusion.

Through their experiences, we learn how to harness the power of diverse perspectives to drive organizational success.

The infinite portfolio is enriched by the contributions of diverse and inclusive teams, reflecting the dynamic interplay between individual and organizational growth. Visionary leaders understand that their portfolios are not limited to their own capabilities but are amplified through the talents and efforts of diverse and inclusive teams. This chapter delves into the ways in which leaders leverage diversity and inclusion to expand their infinite portfolios, driving their organizations toward sustained success.

16

Chapter 16: Sustainability and Environmental Responsibility

Sustainability and environmental responsibility are critical considerations for visionary leaders who seek to create a positive and lasting impact. This chapter explores the importance of integrating sustainability into leadership practices, examining how leaders drive environmental stewardship and sustainable innovation. Through compelling narratives, we uncover the strategies employed by leaders to build environmentally responsible organizations.

Sustainability involves a commitment to minimizing environmental impact and promoting practices that ensure the well-being of future generations. Visionary leaders understand that sustainable success requires a balance between economic growth and environmental preservation. This chapter delves into the stories of those who have championed sustainability within their organizations, highlighting their ability to implement eco-friendly practices and drive sustainable innovation. By examining their approaches, we gain valuable insights into the principles of sustainable leadership.

At the core of sustainability lies the ability to create a culture of environmental responsibility and awareness. Visionary leaders recognize that fostering a sense of environmental stewardship among team members is essential for achieving long-term sustainability goals. This chapter explores the importance of building a culture of sustainability, offering practical insights into the strategies employed by leaders to promote environmental responsibility. Through their experiences, we learn how to create organizations that prioritize sustainability and contribute to the greater good.

The infinite portfolio is enriched by sustainable practices, reflecting the dynamic interplay between innovation and environmental responsibility. Visionary leaders understand that their portfolios must be built on a foundation of sustainability, ensuring that their actions contribute to the well-being of the planet. This chapter delves into the ways in which leaders integrate sustainability into their infinite portfolios, driving their organizations toward responsible and sustainable growth

17

Chapter 17: Legacy and Impact

The legacy of a leader is defined by the lasting impact they leave on their organizations and the world. This chapter explores the concept of legacy, examining how visionary leaders create a lasting impact through their actions and decisions. Through engaging narratives, we uncover the ways in which leaders build enduring legacies that inspire future generations.

Legacy is not solely measured by financial success or accolades; it is defined by the positive change a leader brings to their organization and society. Visionary leaders understand that their true legacy lies in the values they uphold, the lives they touch, and the impact they create. This chapter delves into the stories of those who have left indelible marks on their fields, highlighting their ability to inspire and empower others. By examining their approaches, we gain valuable insights into the principles of legacy building.

At the heart of building a legacy lies the ability to inspire and mentor future generations of leaders. Visionary leaders recognize that their greatest impact often comes from their ability to guide and develop others. This chapter explores the importance of mentorship and succession planning, offering practical insights into the strategies employed by leaders to ensure their legacy endures. Through their experiences, we learn how to cultivate a culture of mentorship and inspire the next generation of innovators and leaders.

The infinite portfolio is a reflection of a leader's legacy, encompassing the ideas, values, and impact they leave behind. Visionary leaders understand that their portfolios must be built with an eye toward the future, ensuring that their contributions continue to inspire and drive progress long after they are gone. This chapter delves into the ways in which leaders build enduring legacies through their infinite portfolios, driving their organizations toward sustained success and positive change.

The Infinite Portfolio: Innovation, Leadership, and the Billionaire's Playbook for Change

In "The Infinite Portfolio," embark on a captivating journey through the multifaceted world of innovation and leadership. This book offers an in-depth exploration of how visionary leaders harness the power of creativity, collaboration, and resilience to drive transformative change. Through a series of engaging chapters, readers are introduced to the stories and strategies of trailblazing entrepreneurs and industry pioneers who have redefined the paradigms of success.

Each chapter delves into a unique aspect of leadership and innovation, from embracing disruption and fostering creativity to navigating the unknown and leading through crises. The book highlights the importance of strategic thinking, ethical leadership, and the power of collaboration in building resilient organizations that thrive in the face of adversity. Readers will gain valuable insights into the art of empowering teams, leveraging technology, and fostering diversity and inclusion to create dynamic and innovative ecosystems.

"The Infinite Portfolio" emphasizes the significance of sustainability and environmental responsibility, guiding leaders to integrate eco-friendly practices into their organizations. It also explores the concept of legacy, inspiring future generations of leaders to leave a lasting impact through their actions and decisions.

With practical insights, real-world examples, and thought-provoking narratives, "The Infinite Portfolio" serves as a comprehensive guide for leaders seeking to build a future defined by innovation, purpose, and positive change. Whether you are an aspiring entrepreneur or a seasoned executive, this book will equip you with the knowledge and inspiration to lead with vision and

CHAPTER 17: LEGACY AND IMPACT

drive meaningful impact in an ever-evolving world.